About the Author

Denny Vasquez is a California educator who received the award for California State Educator of the Year in 2018 for his work within CTE programs such as Robotics, SkillsUSA and student academic achievement. His students have won over 100 awards in various competitions which range from programming to public speaking. He is married to Melissa Vasquez, who is also a phenomenal teacher and has inspired his journey. They have three children and reside in Southern California. He is credited as an exceptional young adolescent educator and motivator whose passion for impacting lives has translated into success within the educational landscape.

The War Within
A Story of Triumph from the California State Educator of the Year

Denny A. Vasquez

The War Within
A Story of Triumph from the
California State Educator of the Year

Olympia Publishers
London

www.olympiapublishers.com
OLYMPIA PAPERBACK EDITION

A CIP catalogue record for this title is
available from the British Library.

ISBN: 978-1-78830-578-5

First Published in 2020

Olympia Publishers
Tallis House
2 Tallis Street
London
EC4Y 0AB

Printed in Great Britain

Dedication

Dad – I can't put into words what you've meant to me. You've been my greatest fan my entire life. It was important for me to tell this story not only for me, but for you. People need to see what your hard work in me has become! Stand up old man... this is your moment just as much as it is mine.

Denise – I love you lil sis. I just want to make you proud to have me as your big brother. I'm always here.

Londa (Mom) – Thank you for accepting the invitation. I know it hasn't always been great, but I want you to know that you helped create a life that I would not have had if it weren't for you. Thank you for treating me like your son. I am proud to call you my mother.

Melissa – I don't want to think about what life would have been like without our little family. You are my greatest inspiration for teaching. Thank you for sticking by my side. I know it isn't easy. I love the life we have made. I just want you to be proud of me.

My Boys – When you get older, I want you to see me for what I have done to help impact this world for good. Just like all the superheroes we watch, I want you to be inspired and unafraid to make decisions that bring joy and positive change to those you come in contact with. My greatest hope is that you know who God is and that he keeps you close to him. I love you.

Family and Friends – Thank you for never leaving me alone. It saved my life.

Acknowledgements

I want to express a sincere thank you to those that I have met in my journey that have helped shape me as a person. Whether it was through sports, friendship or education I'm extremely grateful that our paths have crossed in some way.

To my brother/cousin/friend Aaron and Ryan: You guys were always there for me. I know you felt a need to look after me when everything was falling apart. Even to this day, you are still here. I love you guys with all my heart.

To Dr. Derek King: Thank you for seeing in me that which I didn't see in myself. Thank you for supporting my ambitions as an educator and for always defending my aspirations even when you couldn't see the end result.

Thank you to all the people who helped make this possible for me through all the donations and support. I will not forget it.

August 16th, 1990

I was supposed to go with him. I was supposed to be in that building where everything took place. But for some reason, I chose not to go this time. I'm not sure what feeling I had at the moment either. It was just a spur of the moment decision and I chose not to go with my dad to pick my mom up from work.

It was an everyday thing, picking my mom up. I remember each day that I went inside, the lady at the front desk would give me candy. I was 10. What kid doesn't like candy at 10. I can still smell the scent of old carpet, cigarette smoke outside and aged wood. I would pass by every office and wave to each person inside and smile as they waved back. Everyone in that office seemed to love my mother. Like, love her, love her. She was the pride of her school. Northwest College is what it was. A vocational school where people could earn their nursing and other medical certifications. My mother taught the nursing class which, come to think of it, is actually quite ironic considering how motherly I remember her. She was hard, but extremely passionate. She loved to sing and dance with me on Saturdays as we were cleaning the house. She would often put on Michael Jackson songs and ask me to dance for her because she thought I would be famous one day. She would always say, "Denny, you are gonna do something special one day."

I never understood what possessed that man to do what he did. As a child, I always had very deep thoughts about how he felt after killing my mother. Was he not aware that there were other lives connected to the one he was about to take? Did he not realize how much my beautiful mother meant to me? To her students? To her school? My father told me the story very vividly when he felt that I was able to bear it and, to this day, I see him as the strongest person I have ever met.

My father left to pick up my mother. I stayed home. I was tired. It was summertime and I had stayed up late watching Star Wars, I believe. He explained to me that he pulled up to the school and waited outside until the students were leaving the building. He said that he saw students rushing out of the building and wondered what was happening. I asked him why he didn't go inside earlier and he didn't know why. He heard two loud gun shots in the building and rushed inside. Upon going in, he saw the chaos around him, with people screaming and crying. As he moved toward my mother's room, he looked over to his right and saw my mother lying on the floor. The man had shot her twice in the chest. My father says that my mother tried to stop an argument between a student and her boyfriend. The man and my mother got into an altercation and the man shot my mother and left. My father says that he held my mother in his arms as she was gasping for air. He held his beloved wife, the love of his life, in his hands and watched her life slowly slip away and there was nothing he could do about it. I have thought a lot about that moment. What must it have been like to watch your partner leave this earth without saying goodbye?

My aunt knocked on my door at home. I looked through the peep hole to make sure no one was trying to break in. I had a plan and an escape route if someone did.

I watched a lot of movies. My aunt nervously told me that she was here to pick me up and that my mother was sick. I don't know what possessed her to drive by the school that day. She knew that my mother was not there. I think that she just wanted to see for herself, and I didn't blame her because so did I. There was a lot of yellow tape, policemen and firetrucks at the scene. Lots of people moving around. We were driving very slowly. People were not honking at us. They wanted to see as well. I began to realize that my mother was not sick. Something terrible had happened and I knew that my mother was part of it somehow. We arrived at the hospital, Queen of the Valley Hospital in West Covina, where I was born. Walking into the emergency entrance, I saw lots of people and ambulances everywhere. There were people in the waiting room sitting down. A nurse came to my aunt and asked if she needed help and my aunt explained that we were here to see Carolyn Vasquez. This part is fuzzy to me because I don't remember too much except the fact that they took me into a room with my little sister; she was almost two. We stayed there a while. It seemed like forever. I am pretty sure that my family was deciding who was going to come and tell me the news. After a little while, my dad came in the room. He looked sad. I had never seen him cry before. He looked like he had been crying a lot. He put his arm around me and said that something had happened to my mom. I asked him if she was OK and he began to cry. He simply said, "She's gone, Den. She's gone." I knew what that meant. I've watched plenty of dramas and tv shows where that phrase is used to describe someone who is dead. One of my aunts, some years later, said that she didn't believe that I knew what was happening at the time. The reality was that I knew all too well what was happening. The tears came down my face ferociously as my dad held me up. I knew what all of it meant. I was never going to see her again. Ever. No more kisses on the forehead to say goodnight. No more dancing on Saturdays while she vacuums and I dust. No more ice cream on Wednesdays after school. No more cheers from the stands at my football or baseball games. No more singing Christmas Carols at Christmas. She wasn't going to watch me grow up. It was all gone. To say that I was hurting would be an understatement. I was broken, and realizing that there was nothing I could do to bring her back killed me even further. I looked at my baby sister and knew that she would grow up not knowing our mother's love around her. It killed me to see her cute little face hugging me and my father as we shared this moment alone together. I couldn't help but want her to feel protected.

My emotions were all over the place, as you could imagine. I did not visit my mother's body in the hospital when my father left the room. I didn't want to see her lifeless. That was not her. I was scared to see the one person I loved the most in this world dead and lifeless. It scared me. Instead, my family sent in my cousins. They were my overwhelming comfort. My cousins Aaron, Monica and Alisa came into the room by themselves. I remember my cousin, Aaron, who is a year older than me, embracing me like a big brother as I cried uncontrollably. It felt so good to have them there. To hold me. We all cried very hard in that moment and I remember looking at them all crying and thinking to myself, wow, they loved my mother as much as I did. You never know these things as a kid because kids don't normally share their feelings with each other. The tears and emotion said everything to me and as we slowly began to calm down my cousin Aaron says, "When we grow up, we're gonna find this guy and we're gonna kill him." As you can see, we watched too many Rambo, Arnold and Rocky movies. Nodding in agreement and in rage I replied, "Yes, we will." I am happy to report that we have not killed anyone.

The lead up to the funeral was an overwhelming torment to me. The night that we came home from the hospital, I remember being scared to walk into the house. I began thinking that I would see my mother walk through the house or into my room as a ghost. For almost two years, I slept in my room with the pillow over my head trying to shield myself from the inevitable ghost of my mother waking me up in the night or seeing her walk through the hallway. I remember the day of the funeral, speaking to my father and telling him that I didn't want to see Mom in the casket. He said that it's important to say goodbye. I tried my best to tell him that I didn't want to remember her like that. He finally relented and I spent the entire ceremony outside of the chapel while everyone went inside to say their final goodbyes. There were a lot of people. Way more than could fit in the building that was provided. As the ceremony progressed, there was a man that came outside to visit with me. He was my mom's best friend's son. He was in his twenties, I believe. He sat down next to me and I could feel his awkwardness. He didn't know what to say or how to approach me. He simply asked, "Why are you not inside with everyone else?" And I replied, "Because I don't want to remember my mother dead, with makeup on. My cousins told me what she looked like. That isn't her in there." Nodding his head, he said, "I understand, but if you want to... you can come sit next to us?" I said, "Thank you." He continued to sit as I got up and walked away.

The funeral itself was beautiful. The sea of people who had come to pay their respects was exceedingly overwhelming. Hundreds of people from everywhere. Family from Texas, Los Angeles and Kansas came to show their love for her. Students throughout the years came as well. There was no doubt in anyone's mind that people loved my mom. I do not remember too much after the walk up to the resting place, where my mom was buried, except for this one thing the pastor said when he began speaking. He quoted a scripture from the bible that states," Greater love has no one than this, than to lay down one's life for his friends." (NKJV John 15:13) Looking at him, I began to cry. I remember vividly speaking softly to myself saying, "God, I understand... but why did it have to be her?" That question burned in my soul for a very long time. I felt that this must have been a punishment of some kind. Did I do something wrong that caused all this? What was I going to do after this? How was I supposed to live life without her? I think my dad knew what all this meant for him and, to my own testimony, I can say this: my father's ability to parent rose to a whole new level.

El Je-----------FE / El Capitan

Anyone who has met my father will tell you that he is definitely unique. He has a knack for rubbing people the wrong way sometimes, but deep down and I mean WAY deep… his capacity for love is unquenchable. I think that comes from many things, but most notably his experience with loss and how quickly it can come. After my mother's passing, there was an abrupt change that occurred. He was present in my life before, but not as present as he became. He never showed my sister and I an ounce of stress or worry. He seemed to figure things out on the fly. Things like dinner became very simple. "Hey, Dad, what's for dinner?" I would ask. And he would reply, "Whatever it is, you're gonna eat it, OK?" I never challenged him in those years. I did everything he asked me to do. He shielded me from harm and ridicule. He was constantly on alert and aggravated when people didn't have respect for what we had been through. I remember one instance at a baseball practice where he verbally thrashed a kid for making mom jokes to other players. He didn't tolerate stupidity. Nor did he entertain it. He was the wolf in waiting. The Grizzly Bear ready to consume anything that he felt threatened our way of life and emotional state of being. Deep down, I knew it was a result of everything that had happened. He didn't have patience for people who did not understand. Explaining would take too long. His instant reaction was to show you he's not playing around and doesn't have time to entertain your humor. He had a family to raise. If you didn't understand that, he would let you know. Regardless of how it made you feel. To him, your feelings were irrelevant.

The hardest part for me was going back to school the September after my mother was killed. My father never knew of the things that took place at school because kids don't really tell their parents. I was angry inside and I let my frustration out in many ways. Singing became one of them; basketball was one, and getting into occasional fights in P.E. was another. Anyone that said anything about my mom deserved an instant hand to the face. I was not a bully, but kids began to understand what happened to me and I was not going to allow them to mess with me. I knew this was wrong. I knew I had an emotional problem, but I was really good at hiding it, and up until this book, I don't think my father ever knew I got into a fight... not once. I'm sorry, Dad.

My father was my protector and my teacher. His most absolute rule was RESPECT. It meant and still means everything to him. He taught me the importance of shaking someone's hand and looking them in the eyes when you do it. To always answer with more than just a yes, and to give people the best first impression so they don't think you're an idiot... even if you are. But the greatest lesson that he has taught me, coming out of emotional darkness, is that being able to solve problems is everything in life. There is a specific memory in my mind where I felt the most respect and admiration for my father and, coincidently, it came shortly after my mother's death.

My two uncles, my father and my aunt took me and my three cousins to Mexico for a week. Some people would say to themselves, "Wow that's so awesome!" Let me paint the experience as best as I can. It's 1990. The summer of 1990, mind you. In August. Living in Southern California in August has its perks if you are near water. If you aren't... well... it sucks to be you. My family had the audacious idea to drive to Bahia De Los Angeles from Fontana, California. If you were to Google this now, it says it would take 11 hours. Listen to me when I tell you, it did not take that long. It took longer. We spent about 36 hours trying to get to this place. It took roughly a little less than two days because of car overheating issues, bathroom breaks and the occasional panic to find water. Upon arriving to this place, we quickly realized that we were in the middle of Baja with relatively low human contact around us other than a whale conservation station and a small harbor market. It was a small fishing town. The beautiful part was that we camped on the beach 10 steps from the ocean. We unloaded and setup camp. It was morning and the sand was already hot. My cousins and I were about to run into the water when my uncle shouted, "Don't get in there!" He threw a rock in the water and as we watched it sink, hundreds of sting rays began to scatter. We couldn't get in. One of the biggest let downs of the trip. It was over 100 degrees outside and we could not get wet.

The parents' plan was to fish for our dinner using my uncle's boat and explore the neighboring islands. As the boat was docked, we all climbed in as my aunt stayed behind to prepare the week. My uncle drove the boat for about 45 minutes out into the ocean and around the islands. After about three hours of catching fish, he decided it was time to head back, but there was a big problem. The engine had begun to malfunction and it was not starting. We were approximately 45 minutes off shore, where no one could see us, and our boat was not starting. Now, this is the part where panic began to set in a little for my cousins and I, but what amazes me to this day was the clear head and problem-solving ability of my father, and my uncle. They wasted no time and worked together to try and diagnose the problem. They rowed the big boat for about 15 minutes to one of the nearby islands and tried their best to get it started. After a good 30 minutes, the boat finally kicked back on. They all celebrated giving each other hugs and high fives knowing full well we all could have died that day. What impressed me the most was my father's unrelenting attitude of not giving up. All of them to be honest. The attitude of 'this is going to work' and getting it right until it does work despite everything that's around him. I felt protected. I felt proud and I know they did too. I think at that point, I realized that my family was going to do whatever was necessary in order to help me understand that they were not going to let me down. My father was going to go to whatever length necessary to prove to me that, although life is hard at times, you can always find your way back. He started doing things that he's always wanted to show me. Things like how to start a fire from nothing, cooking, how to lay brick properly, sailing, and even building our very own tree house were some of the things he pursued. I remember being 11 years old and he says to me one day that we are going to go sailing. I thought he meant on a sailboat where someone else was sailing. Nope. He meant what he meant. He was sailing the boat and I was his wingman. I was a great swimmer, but fear was something I had a hard time controlling. I think sailing a hobie catamaran helped me to realize how important your actions and awareness can be. It was always cold, wet and extremely violent at times. For an 11 year old boy to be thrust into a situation like this seems harsh, but my dad understood that if I was going to be a man someday and be able to get through what he has, I was going to need to be challenged in ways that I was not comfortable with.

Over the years, as most kids do, they become resistant to their parents. Although I did what he asked me to do, I also contended with him when I felt that his judgment was not right, but I remember a specific instance where his love for me and his need for my success was brought to the forefront of my future. I had always had dreams of going to UCLA. I applied there, but got denied and hid the letter from my father. I subsequently didn't want to go to school after that and decided I was going to work instead. I thought that my dad would let it go and let me do my thing. Nope. He had other plans. He arranged a meeting with a local university Chancellor to help get me into the school. After much arguing and frustration, I agreed to meet and I was accepted. Although, at the time, I was going through a lot of emotional uncertainty about the direction of my life, my father had a clear idea of the opportunity and life experience that he wanted me to have. Graduating from college was the pinnacle of his life. I could see that he felt a sense of completion at that moment. I couldn't help but think and feel at the graduation ceremony that my mother would have been so proud of me. I also couldn't help but feel some sadness and guilt for not trusting my father enough to realize that he just wanted me to be successful. Not just for myself, but for him and my little sister. For me to succeed would also mean that he also had succeeded. That he had done right by his internal promise to God and my mother to lead me correctly. Little did I know that God wasn't done with me yet. He was going to bring me through fire in order to set me on high, and it was going to hurt.

Changing Professions

I think there are moments in life that solidify how far you've come and where you are going. For me, those days were when I got married and when my three boys were born. Having boys always brings me back to who my father was towards me. He was extremely hard sometimes for no reason, but I ultimately understood why he was the way he was with me. I carry some of his brashness, but my intent is different. I feel like I know where they need to be, but getting there was not always clearly seen. When my wife and I got married, I was working in a marketing agency that provided large format advertising across the United States. My college degree was in marketing so, naturally, that's the career I chose. While working there, I developed great relationships, but it was creating a very hard environment for me because I was driving very far to work and staying long hours.

Hence, the more time I spent at work, the more time my wife had to handle our children. It was in my third year at this marketing agency that God started speaking to me in ways I have a hard time expressing. I had this strong desire to change the world. I wanted to be part of something that would impact people, but didn't know what it was. People would always say join the church, you would be great and maybe I would have been, but I felt that I needed to be part of something bigger. In 2008, the stock market crashed and the economy took a big hit which affected everything in our world at the time. People began to spend less on advertising and I was starting to see it affect my paycheck to the point where I didn't have enough money to even get to work. In my heart, I knew it was time to leave, but I didn't know where I was going to go to find work. My wife was and is a teacher and she has been a great inspiration in my pursuit to teach. However, she went to school for a while and gained a teaching position that way. I didn't have that much time. I needed to do something now. I wondered how long it would take to get into teaching and a friend of mine said that I could actually start substitute teaching if I had a college degree and took a basic math and English test. I took a day off, took the test and applied at the district where my wife worked to make it easier for traveling. I was hired as a substitute teacher in Barstow, California and left the job I was at to pursue a teaching credential. Now, all of that sounds super simple and straight to the point. What I didn't mention was how we didn't have money to pay for our house; I had to sell my truck in order to have money for bills and I hit a 70-pound

Pitbull in the only car we had looking for another job in the meantime. Hitting the dog completely destroyed the front end of the car and I had to borrow money from family just to get the car fixed, and all this time trying to raise two boys who were two and three years old. It was hard. I leaned on God for everything and when I say everything, I mean everything. I prayed so hard and was in my bible so much that it started to rip. He continually promised me that he was going to bring me out of this. I had no money, my wife was constantly upset and asking questions of what we were going to do, bills were due and I couldn't pay them. My hope was slowly going away. I felt my life slowly getting destroyed bit by bit.

I used the financial aid money from school to help offset some of the bills we had and worked all day substitute teaching, and at In N Out burger at night. Kids from school would see me cooking fries at In N Out and say to me, "Hey, aren't you a teacher? Why are you working here?" It was an exhausting life. I felt as though I was stuck and that things were not moving fast enough. After a year and half of this, and finally getting back on our feet a little bit, I was told that I could apply as an intern with a local school district to try and get a position. There was an ad on the radio that said there was going to be a school in the high desert that was going to be hiring teachers for the upcoming school year. They were only selecting two. I felt I had no chance, simply because I wasn't qualified enough. I remember reading a scripture the night before the interview stating that God was going to make a way where there wasn't one. I felt that scripture was for me. I went into the interview that day very confident. Whether I got the job or not, I felt I was moving in the right direction. Upon arriving, I quickly realized my chances of getting the job were extremely slim. There were over 300 people there. I was in the middle. I proceeded through the interview and answered every question as accurate and honest as I knew how. Upon leaving, I was sure that I didn't get the job. I called my wife and told her there were too many people and I don't think I was qualified enough. The moment I said that, I could hear God telling me, "I am bigger than this." About an hour later, I got a call from the human resources department telling me that I got the job. Although I was not qualified to take the position, God gave it to me anyway. It was one of the most joyful times teaching I had up until that point. My family would be able to stay in our home and I was doing what I had worked so hard for. The ironic thing was that this school was a means to a bigger picture because, three months later, I was released from the school as a result of having an invalid intern credential. Apparently, my intern credential was for middle school and not high school or a single subject; therefore, I was let go. I immediately went back to the place of despair that I was all too familiar with. Once again, I had to worry about how I was going to pay for my family's expenses. My wife's income was not enough to cover everything.

The day after I was let go by that school, I immediately looked online for new teaching jobs. To my surprise, a school very close to my home was hiring for a math and science teacher. At the time, teachers were being pink slipped as a result of budget cuts from the state, and school districts were re-hiring to fulfill the teachers they had cut. I told myself that there was no way that God would bring me this far and leave me like this. I also felt that there was no way he could give me two teaching jobs within a four month period when all these other teachers were being let go. I applied for the job at the school near my home through the neighboring school district and received a call that day to set up an interview the following day. I went in, did the interview and was offered the position on the spot. The amount of joy I had was unquenchable. I shook the superintendents' hands, walked out of the interview, went to my car and began sobbing like a baby. This time, I felt it was secure. I was planted. It felt as if I was special to him. All the heartache and disappointment was removed and he was fulfilling his promise to me. Little did I know, there was more in store.

Teaching

It was 2011 and the beginning of my first real teaching position. As a result of the school year starting, I was coming into this new school as the new kid on the block. I didn't know what to expect other than the same middle school vibe of disobedience amongst adolescence. The principal at the time had told me that the classes that I was going to be taking over had been changing teachers every couple of weeks since the school year started. I knew instantly what that meant. It meant that the students would not accept me as their teacher unless they were absolutely sure I was going to stay. Now, my methods of winning students do not involve elaborate educational knowledge or extremely great teaching skills. My gift, I believe, is who I am and where I come from. My story seems to cut deep with students when I explain it to them. The very first day of school there were faculty coming to me saying that the students I have are terrible and I'm going to have a hard time. They gave me all of the teaching materials necessary with example lesson plans and helpful strategies in order to teach the kids what they need to know. As a teacher, I felt that what they gave me was important. As a man and human being, I felt that what was more important was for them to know who their teacher was and that I was not leaving them.

The first day, I clipped all of the paperwork and lesson plans that were given to me all together in one pile. I placed a stool at the front of the class, wrote my name on the board and waited for them to knock. In my classroom, I prayed to God asking him to give me the words to speak that would change their hearts and minds to be for me and not against me. When I didn't hear a knock, I opened the door to see where they were. The security guard was standing next to the students as they lined up outside my door. I had never seen such a thing. The students all came in giggling and looking at me in curiosity and ridicule. The security guard came into the classroom and sat in the back. I quickly told him that I had this under control and that I didn't need his assistance. He assured me that I did and that he was going to stay. I said OK and immediately sat down on the stool looking at each of the students with great sincerity. I told them my name and that I wanted to share my story with them in hopes that they would understand where I am coming from, and that I want desperately to be the best teacher they've ever had. I began telling them my story just as I have to you who are reading this. Beginning with my mother. Within the first five minutes of telling my story, students began to become interested and uncomfortable at the same time. It was obvious that what I was doing was causing an extremely emotional reaction... in a good way. The security guard was looking at the kids in astonishment because they individually began to cry and feel remorse. He got up and left the room. The kids didn't even notice. I continued the story explaining to them that in life there are things you cannot explain at the time. It turned out that there were many students within that class that had lost someone close to them. After I was done telling the story, I explained to them that if they gave me the opportunity that I would do everything in my power to ensure that they are successful at what I'm trying to teach them. But, in turn, I was going to need their full cooperation in order to make it a reality. I did the same thing with the other five classes that I had. At the end of the day, there was a staff meeting where I was introduced as the new teacher on campus. The security guard who was in my classroom told the principal what I did and the principal acknowledge me during the meeting saying he was thankful to have me at the school. From then on, those students were mine and I was theirs and there was nothing that was going to change that. We spent the entire school year learning with each other. I would teach a lesson, finish it and ask them, "What did you guys think? Did you understand, or do we need to do that again a different way?" They were all honest with me. They would say Mr. Vasquez that sucked bad and you need to do that again, or they would say that it was great and they wanted that style of teaching. After a few weeks, I found my groove and things started moving really fast. I would not have been able to do it had it not been for a mentor teacher, Sherrie. She helped me develop great strategies that I still use to this day. Together in our math collaborations, we developed strategies that would help the students achieve better scores on their California State tests. In my final year at the school, we raised our schools scores by almost 26 percent which was 20 percent higher than any other middle school in the district. We implement a reward strategy that involved specific rewards for students that involved things they loved like video games, sports, movie days and free time. It all promoted learning because the students knew their reward was real. I learned so much at that school, but the saying 'nothing lasts forever' was an understatement.

Robotics

Towards the end of my first year at the school, I was approached by the principal to take over an advanced elective call Paxton Patterson Lab. This lab had all the bells and whistles with regards to S.T.E.M. at the time. Everything from a dedicated computer lab with Autodesk and Programming software to a drill press and experimental equipment. I had no formal training but, apparently, I looked like the right guy for the job. He had explained that there were 20 classroom VEX Robotics kits in portables in the back of the school that were not being used. I asked him if I could take one of them home and build something that maybe the students could build themselves. He said yes and my sons and I (who were six and a half and two) started to build a test bot at home. I followed the instructions, made the robot and was able to control it with the remote provided. I came back to school the next day and placed the example bot on a table and said we are going to build robots for the rest of the school year. That summer, I was sent to Cal Poly Pomona's Project Lead the Way camp to learn how to use STEM within the classroom. The training was very intense and rigorous. I was able to finish and left there with some knowledge of how to use programming to help the students. I looked up VEX Robotics because I had heard at the training that there were competitions where the students could test themselves and their builds against others who do the same thing. We turned the class into a competition class where the students built robots specifically to compete. We went to our first competition and got completely destroyed. It was an eye opener to say the least. I expected the students within that class to tell me that they wanted to stop going to competition. In fact, it was the opposite and began working really hard to try and win. We researched ways to improve by searching for videos and mechanisms of VEX Robotics competition online and tried to mimic their builds. We built things and took them down and continued to do so for quite a while. Through all of this, I was learning how the components of VEX Robotics worked and how we could use them to help make ourselves better. That year, we did not achieve much in the area of hardware (trophies), but I gained some valuable experience and started to understand the competitiveness that is VEX Robotics.

I became extremely passionate about trying to help make the students successful in this area so, the following year, I researched more competitions that we could possibly attend. In the process of asking questions, I was approached by my assistant principal at the time to pursue a competition called SkillsUSA which I knew nothing about. He explained to me that it was a student led organization that allowed the kids to compete in many different types of competitions, which included Robotics and Public Speaking. That year, I made it my focus to try to not only impact the students' lives in a positive way but to also give them something to feel confident about. It was my mission. I had to do this. I spent very long nights watching videos on YouTube and listening to lectures on mechanical engineering, of which I knew nothing about. We did better than the year before which was great, but the more important aspect of it all was that the students were being challenged academically, emotionally and technically. They started to understand the importance of being prepared. We began to have a plan each day and set goals as to what we wanted to accomplish with clear lines of sight on how to get to where we wanted to be. I was flourishing as an educator and as a byproduct of my development, and so were they. It was not hard to see, but then it all came to an emotional halt.

Within the district I was working in, there were rumblings of another budget cut that would remove some teachers from their classrooms on the basis of seniority. Board meetings began to happen where voting took place to implement this action in order to save the district from receiving punishment from the State of California. As a result of me only working in the district for two years, naturally, I was one of the lowest on the list. The thoughts of reliving what I had previously gone through were on the forefront of my mind. My wife was worried that we would be in the same position we were in previously because of what was about to happen. The sad part about it all is the events of the budget cut took away from the fact that my students advanced to the State Championship and won in their SkillsUSA contest and moved on to Nationals. They were State Champions. And, yet, the fact that I was going to lose my job was the hardest part to bear. A week before the decision to let teachers go, there was a board meeting that was held at a local high school in order to finalize the voting and move forward with the decision. I wanted to attend the meeting to see what they would be discussing. I had never gone to a school board meeting before. It was chaos. There were a lot of angry parents and people whispering everywhere. As I received the agenda for the meeting, I realized quickly that I was one of the speaking topics of the meeting. Parents and faculty from the school had come together to try to persuade the board to make an exemption for me regarding the layoffs. There were a lot of reasons and statistics given in order to give reasoning, but it seemed that the board had already made up their minds. There were three of the seven that had voting against letting me go. Majority ruled and the layoffs commenced. I remember getting called into the front office of the school and meeting with the human resources superintendent at the time. All I remember was the smile he had on his face. It offended me. It was a representation of the lack of RESPECT my father always told me to have. He did not care about the impact that I made on the students, how many lives I had changed or the improvement in test scores and academics. To him, I was another teacher that had to receive the slip and he had a job to uphold. I took the slip respectfully and remember him saying to me, "Thank you for everything you've done Mr. Robot Man." I will never forget that.

Some weeks had passed and I was starting to prepare for the end of the school year with the students. We accepted a project I received as a result of the success we had had throughout the year from an organization called STSI (Space Telescope Science Institute). They wanted to know if we would be interested in building a scale model of the James Webb Space Telescope that would be launched in the year 2018. I happily accepted and the kids and I built a model for the institute that I believe is still there to this day, if I am not mistaken. We spent two months constructing it and created a video for them to see. It was a nice going away gift to the students because it allowed me to spend some quality time before I left the school.

Towards the end of the project, I received a phone call from another school asking if I would be interest in talking to him about starting up a Robotics program at a new school. Although I was losing my job, I was informed by human resources that there was a possibility, not certain, that I could be hired back into the same position that I currently was in when the numbers came back. The man, Derek King, was the new principal at a school called Excelsior's Aviation, Medicine and Engineering Academy. To this day, I thank God for him. He was a bright light in a very sad time for me. He had watched everything that had taken place during the board meetings and had been following the students' success in the newspapers, and through word of mouth. At first, I told him I had to think about it because I honestly didn't trust it was all going to go through but, if you know Derek, you know that he is all in when he knows what he's after. A couple days later, he called me again asking if I had given it any thought and I told him that I would like to meet because I wanted to let him know the cost involved in starting a program like what I had, let alone being successful at it. He agreed and we sat down to discuss everything. I explained to him that I felt very confident that I could build a great program if we had all the tools necessary to be successful, but the most important thing I needed was time. I wanted more time with the students. In a traditional school, time is based on scheduling and the periods were only 50 minutes. I told him that it's not possible to compete with the higher performing competitive teams when you are only given 40 minutes to build something a day. He said that he could make it work and that he would give me a call closer to the beginning of the school year to set up an interview with the Superintendents of Excelsior.

Excelsior was, and is, a charter school that works as a hybrid independent study program. The students have seat time in class, but also have the option of doing their work independently if they so choose. This meant I would have up to two hours of build time with the students after their core classes. In addition, it was a '7 thru 12' school, which meant that I could have the same students from the time they were in 7th grade all the way up to 12th grade, and facilitate their learning in a more hands on way. Once I knew the details, I was all in. In July of 2013, I received a call from Excelsior to come for an interview. I left the interview extremely confident. I spoke to my wife and said, "I think I got the job." Derek called me an hour later and said, "Congratulations and welcome to the team." I was ready.

A.M.E. Robotics

In the first week at my new school, I wondered how in the world I was going to do what I said I could do. We literally started with nothing. There were no desks, no chairs, no whiteboards, no computers and the VEX Robotics Equipment was in boxes. As the students came in, all I could think was, "Every parent is going to take their kid right out of this school." And, to be honest, some did. But I told the incoming students that this was going to be their school, their team and their classroom. I explained that they were going to be the ones who started everything. The ones that looked forward to it accepted that challenge and helped me build something special.

The first year was all business. I didn't entertain the kids with great stories or facts about my life. I felt that if I wanted to create a serious program that would contend with the best, I had to not only act like it but I had to embody it. I printed a slogan on t-shirts that no one had really heard of back then but it said, "Hard work beats talent when talent doesn't work hard." It was everywhere and it became the answer to every rebuttal that the students had when it came to their work, their robot builds and even their teams. As soon as the school year started, I entered the students into competitions both local and outside of our area. Now that we had two hours of build time, I started by building something that the kids could mimic themselves. It wasn't advanced, but it was more than they were expecting and so they began modeling and modifying my build to things they felt would work. We had a field test in our classroom which was like the real thing which made it easier to see if their designs worked. If it didn't, they would immediately go back and rework their designs to better fit the problems of the game. VEX Robotics is a competitive sport. It challenges students to get outside their comfort zones and improve on their ability to communicate, problem solve and use real world thinking to make decisions. The game changes every year with new tasks and problems that the students need to solve within a 1 min and 45 second period. The first 15 seconds are autonomous where the robot tries to gain points based on a code that automates the movements of the robot. The remaining time is used as a driver control period where the robot has be programmed to a joystick and the students drive the robot to gain the remaining points. Each match, there are four people on the field: two opponents and one alliance team. The alliance team and your team try to outscore your opponents by solving the different problems on the field. Whoever has the most points at the end of the match wins.

We were not good at first. We spent the entire first year just trying to stay above water and compete without something falling off during a match. I remember seeing the frustration on the students faces after going to competition on Saturdays wondering why their robots didn't work. It frustrated me because I didn't intervene like most teachers would have. I let the students endure the hostility and the lack of judgement with regards to the robot because I knew if I built everything, the students would not achieve the necessary skills in order to become great at this. So I watched. In complete and utter anguish as we lost match after match. I doubted whether or not what I was doing had any benefit and then a few weeks before the playoffs of our last league competition, a group of students built something that actually worked quite well. It just needed some modifications. I suggested the modifications to the high school team and middle school teams that were attending the playoffs and they built the robot and tested it in the field. It worked. It worked so well, in fact, that the kids were shocked that it did. The final week, we practiced every single day for almost three hours. I contacted the parents and told them that they needed to finish all of their work and turn it in to their facilitators so that we had more time to practice. The two students, Kyndal and Xavier were both 7th graders with no prior experience. They were both shy and spoke to no one unless spoken to and even then the response was very minimal. I felt in my heart that this "thing" they were doing called Robotics was going to change them. I felt compelled to do it. The high school team also completed the same robot and took it as well after seeing the progress made.

Walking into the auditorium, we had no idea what was about to take place, nor did any of us understand what it was going to mean for the future of that school year. All we wanted to do was to try to win. The ironic and most devastating thing about it all was who we were playing against. My previous school, with my previous students, had entered into the competition as well and my old friend Sherrie was their new coach. I loved those kids and appreciated Sherrie so much for taking over the program and not letting it fall. There was joy and pain all at once as I watched my new students gain the last few points to win the championship of the tournament against my old school. They had both reached the finals and had to play against each other to win it all. After winning and seeing my former students crying, I rushed over to them to give them a hug and to let them know that I loved them. It hurt a lot. I walked over to my current students and congratulated them on winning and was informed that we had qualified for the State and National Championship. We were going to Omaha, Nebraska, to play against some of the best teams in the world. There were so many emotions happening all at once. We were going to experience the best that VEX had to offer and all I wanted to do was learn everything I could to get better. We placed fifth at the State Championship and fifth at the National Championship and came home with our heads held high. We proved to ourselves that we could compete, and the pride of our school rose.

But there was also a different side to all of this. There were students who had embraced the slogan and embraced who I was and what I meant to them, but didn't achieve what the others had achieved. They were happy for the ones that did advance and get to travel, but were sad that it didn't happen to themselves. One student in particular, Bryce, was dealing with some turmoil at home that had caused a more subdued and quiet demeanor. He was not talkative. Nor was he flashy. He came to school, stayed till the last minute and then caught the bus to go back home. He never missed a day of school. He was always there to listen, and was ready to be taught and then, one day, he came to me demanding something. His story reminded me of my own. He didn't have a father present in his life. His mother had a boyfriend, but that man was not what he was looking for. He wanted a role model and someone he could count on to always tell him the right thing to do. He craved it. He came to me one day and said, "Mr. Vasquez, I want you to teach me everything you know. I want to know everything you know about life and how to handle all of it. I want to learn from you and make good decisions like you do." I was really shocked by this because it was unexpected, but I knew he was serious. So I accepted his request and began to have a more direct role in his daily life. I started treating him like my own sons, holding him accountable for his decisions and letting him know the consequences of them, good and bad. After losing in robotics, we entered into SkillsUSA's competition season and he and another student, Cody, began to win as middle schoolers in an all high school public speaking contest. At the State Championship, Bryce became the first middle schooler to win the California State SkillsUSA Championship in Job Skill Demonstration against high schoolers with Cody coming in third as an 8th grader. Bryce would go on to the National Championship that year to place 6th amongst high schoolers as an 8th grader.

In the years following our first year, we experienced great loss. We were not able to repeat any of the previous successes within the VEX Robotics platform. For a period of two years, the students tried supremely hard, myself included, to replicate some form of success that we attained in our inaugural season. There were many doubts that crept in throughout this time and I wondered if there would be any form of success that my students could carry with them. Then in my third year of being at A.M.E., a kid named Adam arrived.

Adam had come to visit the school a year before to take a tour and I remember thinking to myself, "I think this kid is scared of me." Then, after speaking to him and his parents, Jennifer and Mike, I realized that this was not a regular 6th grader. Adam was a kid with extreme intelligence, specifically in the area of computer programming. He was always prepared and never late. He was the kid who exceeded expectations when there weren't any to begin with and, yet, I still sensed that he wanted a teacher he could belong to who accepted him for who he was. Different. He was mature beyond his years at 12 and, because of that, he did not relate well to students with a less mature approach to schoolwork and competition. Yet, as the school year progressed, his sense of humor began to shine and he became one of the cornerstones of our program. Everyone leaned on him for advice and input because they valued his straight forward opinion. In his first year of being at our school, he helped his team achieve mild success by winning matches, but nothing on a level that he would say he was happy with. He was kind and extremely polite. He shied away from confrontation, but wasn't afraid to bring up points of interest that he felt were important. This was never more evident until the day that Colin showed up the following year.

Colin was the complete opposite of Adam, in every way possible, but his ability to build and maneuver parts with his hands was very obvious amongst his peers. He was not easy to get along with and introducing him to the team was both an exciting time and a challenging one because I saw an opportunity. I understood what Colin could mean to a team that had complementing pieces. I wanted the teams within my program to have three essential parts that would ensure the success of the whole: a programmer, a mechanical engineer and a driver. Another student, Jacob, proved to be an exceptional driver of any robot that he possessed. I tested his abilities against the high school teams and even they were astonished by his skills. I created a middle school team, 7209E, that would embody these features. The only problem was that the personalities within the team clashed so much that they argued the entire time they were together. For four months they bickered, cried, yelled and defied each other on the most absolute of levels. It wasn't until the Championship of the High Desert League that they actually understood what they could be.

February 4th, 2017

This day presented a difficult challenge because we had advanced to the championship of the California High Desert League in Hesperia, California and were also competing 15 minutes down the road at the SkillsUSA Region 6 Championship in Apple Valley. Adam, Colin and Jacob were competing in a team engineering challenge within SkillsUSA at 8am and had to be at the VEX Competition by 930am. We pleaded with the Judges of SkillsUSA to have the students compete early so that they could leave and make the other competition in time. They agreed and were able to do as we had hoped. As an advisor to SkillsUSA I had to stay with the group that was still competing while the junior high students left to the VEX competition. While at the awards ceremony for SkillsUSA, the rest of the students and I watched a live video feed of one of the parents watching the playoffs take place. All of us looked on as the students won round after round in convincing fashion. We would give each other high fives as they won each contest. One gentleman came up and asked, "What game are you watching?"

I quickly replied, "We are watching my students try to win a robotics championship for the first time!"

As they proceeded to the finals, we all gathered round in excitement and anticipation. As the final match sounded and the scores were tallied, we could see Colin, Jacob and Adam with smiles on their faces giving each other high fives and shaking their alliances hands as they walked away. We knew they had done it. They had won the California High Desert League Championship and it felt so good. The more important element to the championship was the fact that it showed them that they could achieve anything they worked hard for. Despite their differences, they knew the common goal and worked together to gain what they all wanted. As a result of winning, they received an invitation to the California State Championship which we had not been to since my first year at the school. The students and I were excited to compete, but we all knew that we needed a new robot to compete with the higher level teams. The current design was too slow and took too long to score objects. We had a specific design in mind and in the coming weeks we made our decision... we began to build... Eleanor.

Eleanor

The day after winning the League Championship, I remember being at home watching Avengers thinking to myself how easily Tony Stark was able to not only formulate technology in his head, but also what the purpose of the technology was. For years, I had developed ideas for robots based on the task at hand, but not seeing the ideas for any more than that. Things like improved speed and calculated movements to targets never came to mind. After watching the movie, I realized that Tony's ability to be successful wasn't solely based on the technology alone. He completed tasks more efficiently and more quickly than his competition. I started to visualize movements that our robot would need to have in order to, not only compete against the best in the world, but also do everything faster than them. In the world of VEX Robotics, seconds come at a premium. If you can complete an action faster than your competition, mathematically, you can put the game out of reach before it even starts. Our issue with the current robot was that the lift did not have enough torque or speed to throw the objects over the playing field bars with great speed. This particular game was called Starstruck. The object of the game was as follows: the first 15 seconds of each match was an autonomous period in which the robot is programmed to score points on its own without user assistance. The remaining minute and thirty seconds was user controlled and it was up to the driver of the team to score as many points as possible before time ran out. There were yellow "jacks", if you will, on the playing field as well as three large bean bags on both sides of the playing field. The purpose of the game was to throw the playing objects across the fence located in the center of the field to your opponent's side. The team with the most points after a match wins. The issue was that the bean bags were a bit heavy for VEX motors to lift and overtime, the motors would overheat causing the internal mechanism of the motor to send a signal to the cortex initializing a shut off sequence for 5-7 seconds for cooling. This was detrimental to most teams because the game was very high paced and any time lost was extremely valuable. I started to research mechanical gear methods in the real world that could handle both speed and torque distribute without any lag. I also wanted a drivetrain for the students that allowed them to move about the field more efficiently. Movements with our current drive took too long and there was a lot of wasted time in between gathering objects. The other aspect of the robot that needed improvement was the object grabbing capability. We were very limited in the amount of objects that could be picked up due to the size of the claw that the students had previously built. In addition, the motors would always overheat as a result of the students pressing the button and holding the motors on to keep grasp of the objects in the claw. None of it was efficient. I found a gear box called a planetary gear which had rarely been used in VEX at the time (if ever). It would require the use of six motors on our lift, but the motors would act as a counterbalancing system when certain motors failed. This would not only give us the power and speed we needed, it would also stop us from overheating during matches which would make our ability to score more efficient. VEX only allows for 10 motors to be used on the robot, but upon further inspection of the rules, it stated that we could use 10 motors plus two pneumatic pistons as well. We decided to ditch the motors on the claw and replace them with dual acting pneumatic pistons in order to not only grab the objects, but hold them in place within the claw at 100 psi. We also increase the size of the claw and had it tucked into the robot on a movement based release system that allowed the claw to come down at the beginning of the match. This was important for sizing because we needed to stay within the size limit of 18"x18"x18". When the match started, the robot could extend beyond that point. We also created a "holonomic" drive for the robot which allowed it to move in virtually any direction which removed the robots traditional linear movement and replaced it with a more intuitive "direct to the object" approach. I gave the plans to the students and said, "we have two weeks to do this." I spoke to their parents and told them that we were going to be spending seven-eight hours a day to finish the project and to ensure that when they got home that their schoolwork was finished. I was amazed by the team's willingness to take on the challenge to say the least. It is not easy to get 11-12 year olds to care about something so complex, but I was astonished at how well they complemented each other in their work ethic. I sat back and watched as all three of them spent countless hours building and testing their creations in the most meticulous way. As the robot began to come together, it was extremely obvious that it was going to do what it had intended. The excitement and impatience to complete the finished product began to overwhelm them so much that there were times when I had to intervene and remind them to make the robot as perfect as possible. They finished it with around six days to spare before the state championship. I remember the first test very vividly because it wasn't the fact that they had completed the robot that had amazed me. It was the fact that the robot did more than we had expected and the students were not amazed by its qualities. They knew that their creation's craftsmanship was of the highest level and that they had done it all by themselves. I gave them the idea and they ran with it. It was a satisfying moment to say the least. I smiled as the robot not only grabbed one but two bean bags with ease. It was picking up three "jacks" at a time which was something we never could do before. Jacob's driving ability coupled with the robot's movement was seamless and we could see that he loved it. She was beautiful, Eleanor, and everyone knew it.

2017 California State VEX Robotics Championship (Pomona)

Driving to the event, I wondered what it would mean to the students if they won. What if they won? Imagine? All that hard work they put in. The fights. The attention to detail. The arguing. It would have all been washed away and even at that moment while walking up to check into the State Championship, it was all gone. We had made it back after almost four years of nothing. The robots at the event all looked amazing. We knew it was going to be extremely difficult to win. As the kids unpacked the robot, and brought it to the practice arena, I could see their faces very clearly. They weren't scared. They were anxious. The anticipation of the first match was unbearable. I remember walking up to our driver, Jacob, and asking him, "How do you feel?" He looked at me with a shy gaze and said, "I just want to play." I laughed, patted him on the back and said, "you'll get your chance soon enough." As the matches began, I looked on in both astonishment and nervousness as Eleanor began to win match after match. She was moving and scoring with extreme ease. We moved up the rankings and halfway through the competition we were in first place. The kids couldn't believe it. I couldn't believe it. But just as quickly as our confidence was gained, it was immediately shot down. Upon the loading up for our next qualifying match before playoffs, one of the steel shafts connecting the gears to each other and the motors of the planetary gears had come lose and dislodged itself from the motor. The match started and Jacob could not lift the arms of the robot to throw the objects over the bar. We lost. Consequently, our ranking dropped and we moved into third place.

The way that the playoff system worked at that time was that you had a three team alliance which was gathered through a process called alliance selection. Teams ranked 1-8 would have a chance to pick their alliance member from the list of teams at the competition. Once all eight teams had picked, the choice would come back around to the number one team in order to pick their third and final alliance. As a result of us being in third place, we were able to pick a quality first. In addition, our third alliance was also very good. When all the teams had finished their picks, the students went back to their pit areas and began to game plan with their new playoff alliances in order to try and win the state championship. Kids, mentors, parents and teachers were all gathering around their teams trying to come up with strategies in order to qualify for the VEX Robotics World Championship. To be honest, that was all that mattered to us. The rules stated that you had to make it to the finals of the State Championship, not win, in order to advance to the World Championship. This meant that six teams were going to be awarded invitations to the World Championship if they made it to the finals of the State Championship. We wanted it so bad, but there were others that wanted it just as bad and were going to do whatever was necessary in order to gain it.

Playoff matches started and we began our climb. We beat the first round of playoff alliances pretty convincingly and moved on to the quarterfinal round. We defeated the next team in the same fashion and moved on to the semifinals where were met up with the second place team and their alliance, Team Obvious. We had watched their match prior and noticed that they were having issues with their robot and were not only using the timeouts available to them, but also challenging calls from the referee in order to gain more time to fix the issues with their robot. In addition to this, one of the team members from their team had been watching the number one alliances' matches and noticed that they were committing a very small infraction to the rules listed in the gaming manual. The number one alliance was made up of one team member. He did not have any teammates. His brother had his own robot and was on his alliance. The rules state that no one person can compete on two different teams at any competition which also meant that you couldn't stand with another team, even if you weren't driving the robot. Team Obvious saw this happening and used it to not only disqualify the number one alliance from the tournament, but they also used it to gain additional time to fix their malfunctioning robot. I cannot describe the agony and sadness on that student's face as they were disqualified from the competition. It was clear that he was not helping his brother physically, but was just there for moral support. I was upset that the referees couldn't see that the incident was misjudged and just asked the student not to stand with his brother for the remainder of the tournament. But, as a result of the infraction, it was not only his team that was disqualified, but also his brother's robot and the third alliance who was also disqualified.

As the semifinal match began, we knew we had to make sure the robot worked in all phases. The plan was to have our team and our second pick play first. As the autonomous period began, and the robots started to gain momentum, the amount of anxiety and nervousness was overwhelming. As the final horn sounded, and the scores were tallied, the victory was given to us. A sigh of relief set in, but we knew that it wasn't over. The playoff matches are a best of three which meant we needed to win just one more match and we were going to the World Championship. As the rules had stated, one robot could stay on the field for all three matches, but the other two alliances members had to trade. We chose to sit out the second match and let the other two finish the job. The team ended up losing the second match and which meant that we had to play a third match to decide who was moving onto the finals. The students made sure everything was working and that we were ready to go. As the autonomous buzzer sounded, the match began and the robots started to move. Objects were being tossed in both directions and it was very clear the autonomous period was going to be close. As the horn for autonomous sounded and the judges tallied the score, the autonomous round was awarded to our team. A loud cheer came from the crowd as the user control portion had begun. As the drivers moved around the field scoring objects and defending the other teams assaults, I could feel the anxiety and adrenaline within my body rising to my shoulders and into my neck. It was almost unbearable how much this was going to mean for our school, the students and their families. The final buzzer sounded and the judges tallied the score. The students waited in anticipation for the score to be displayed on the jumbotron on the arena. When the score went up, it was absolute jubilation. We had won. Everyone in the crowd had begun to celebrate as I rushed to the students to give them a hug, but sudden astonishment became prevalent when we had learned that Team Obvious was contesting the final score of the match. The students from their team and ours were gathered around the referee as Team Obvious demanded that the referee had made a mistake and that autonomous was calculated wrongly. The students, the families, myself and the people from neighboring schools all stood in bewilderment and confusion as the referee began to formulate a plan of action. Parents began to yell and scream from stands stating, "The kids won fair and square!" I had recorded the match on my camera and ran to the referee to show him that the playing field clearly showed that we had won the autonomous period. He explained to me that he couldn't take video evidence from the match and that the only other recourse was to replay the match. In as calm a voice as I possibly could muster, I said, "How is that fair when you've already posted the score and shown the students that they've won? You can't complain about the final score of the Superbowl and demand the game be replayed. It's not logical." Nevertheless, he did not listen to me or the screaming parents from the crowd and had decided to replay the match. My students were heartbroken. I tried my best to encourage them and give them hope, but I believe the emotional build up to the match, the fact they won and that it was taken from them brought extreme emotional withdrawal on their part. The match was replayed. We lost and Team Obvious went on to win the California State Championship. I was heartbroken, emotionally destroyed and angry that my students had to go through this. To say they were sad is not even the word. The tears came down very hard that day and there was no amount of consoling that would have replaced what had happened. We felt cheated and robbed at the same time and to watch to kids who had done it raise the State Championship banner in joy was even worse. The saying that 'grown men don't cry' did not apply to me. I cried for most of the car ride home that evening. I thought about my whole life being such a struggle to find meaning and purpose. In my mind, I had this vision that winning the championship and sending my students to World Championship was going to prove to me that I could make a difference in the world somehow and that the success was going to fulfill so much for me. Instead, my students and I were left with nothing but pain and misery. I cancelled robotics for an entire week after that. I couldn't bear to see their faces and Eleanor because it meant that we had to discuss it and it was just too new. Maybe all this emotion was a by-product of my childhood and suppressing memories that were difficult to handle. I just didn't want to be emotionally challenged in that way and I ran from it.

The week after had passed, we came together to talk and decided we were not going to forget what happened, but that we were going to ensure that it didn't happen again. We got invited to the US Open National Championship again that year as a result of our placing throughout the season and it was a good closure to an extremely emotional season. We placed eighth at the National Championship and received the Bracket Buster award for being the lowest seed to defeat the highest seed in the competition (16 seed beating two seed). We competed in other competitions that year within SkillsUSA as well and advanced to the National Championship, but there was something different and special that trickled through the entirety of my team from middle school all the way up to high school. It wasn't just the middle schoolers who had seen all of this take place that year. It was all of my students. They all witnessed the effort and attention to detail that it took to go so far and have it just taken from them. It created a spark in them.

Towards the last days of school, we all gathered in my classroom to clean up and put things away. The emotion was pretty heavy. Words of past failures and achievements came pouring in and the topic of being great became the focus. I told the students that I wanted this next year to be the greatest year we've ever had together. I wanted them to understand and prove to themselves that they were good enough. To be quite fair, I feel as though I was speaking to myself in that moment, but I wanted them to understand how much their success meant to me as well as them. Meaning, we couldn't do it without each other. We had to find a way and commit to it. Whatever it took. It was time....and we all knew it.

2018

The new VEX games are revealed during the festivities at the VEX World Robotics Championship in April every year. In previous years, we haven't begun production of any robots because students are normally at school in the summer or in the early weeks of the school year. This year, we decided that we were going to conceptualize things a bit at the end of the school year and come ready to build the first day of school. There was a purpose to our builds and the vision seemed perfectly clear. This year's game was called, 'In the Zone'. The object of the game was the same from a timing standpoint but this time we had to stack cones on mobile goals and move those stacks to specific zones on our side of the field. There were also stationary goals that we had to stack cones on as well. The object was to not only stack the cones, but to win the high stack bonus by being the highest stacked mobile goal in a specific zone. This time instead of me illustrating the design, the students and I gathered in the field on the first day of school and went over the game rules and important pieces to focus on. We then learned from our previous mistakes and cut right to the chase: what mechanism did we need in order to grab the objects and stack them faster than other teams we were playing against. We seemed a bit confused on the design we wanted on the first day so I told the students that we needed a break and to come back the next day with even more focus. I remember going home that day not thinking about the robot at all. I drove home praying in the car asking God to give my students and I wisdom to make the right decisions throughout the year in order to give the students success because they needed to know what it felt like. I believed that God would bless me again if my effort and commitment to the students and to my craft was genuine and full of hard work. The next day, we came up with a very simple design that, still to this day, is mind blowing how successful it became. The truth about it was that it wasn't flashy, it didn't have a planetary gear or crazy complex user controls or drivetrains. It simply did the job, but moved faster than any robot on the field.

Iris

Iris was made within a one week period. I think some people would say that you couldn't possibly make a championship level robot in such a short amount of time, but I think the difference was that we didn't waste time making something that we weren't going to use. And I say 'we', but it was the students that built it. Ironically, it was the students who had lost all those years ago, Bryce and Cody, who had been waiting to finally make their mark. Iris was a built using six motors on the drivetrain using a small chain on the back two motors to increase consistency between the rear motors for quicker takeoff. The lift was a standard 1 to 1 ratio gear train and the mobile goal intake was modeled after a scooping mechanism used to pick up trash. The pincher or pickup device was two pneumatic pistons that were similar to Eleanor's, but ergonomically formed to the shape of the cones we were picking up. In the first initial tests, the robot was able to stack three-four cones. We made some adjustments and got the stack height up to seven cones. Heading into our first league play match, we weren't sure how it was all going to work out. We hadn't played any other teams except our own and to our surprise, there was a familiar team that had decided to join the league we were competing in. Team Obvious had registered at the league we have been going to for the past five years. We had never seen them this far before and wondered why they would travel so far to compete. Initially, I would say that there was some hostility because all of my students were there the day the middle school team was robbed of their World Championship opportunity, so I didn't need to remind them who Team Obvious was. They knew full well who they were competing against and the type of competitors they were. It became a competition within a competition. Our records were the same throughout the whole three months of the league. Iris was clearly seen as one of the best robots at the competition alongside Obvious.

There was a period of downtime in the month of November where we did not have competition. That gap in competitiveness was replaced by extreme sadness. My grandmother had passed away the first week of April which was hard on my entire family. The following week, a fellow teacher and friend from at our school, Terry Trebilcock, had passed away suddenly from a heart attack. He was so loved by the students and staff at our school that the news was extremely impactful. As you could imagine, I had a hard time dealing with death to begin with and what comes with it. Our entire school staff went through a period of counseling to help cope with the emotional repercussions of his death. School resumed after a few days of the campus being closed and, about two days after resuming practice sessions for robotics, we got word that Cody's, Iris' driver, grandfather had passed away suddenly as well. There was so much emotion happening at one time that it caused practice to be extremely hard. There was less talking and a lot more frustration. Driving wasn't as crisp and tensions were extremely low because no one wanted to ask if everything was ok. We knew it wasn't and yet we were so close to winning our first tournament. The day before the competition, I asked Cody's mother if he was OK and she simply said that he wanted to win the tournament for his grandfather and that he would be there. Once again, I prayed for victory. I prayed for victory for a long and emotional journey.

When it came time for the playoffs and alliance selection, Obvious and our school were numbers one and two respectively. We did not know whether or not, as the number one seed, they would pick us as their alliance so we made plans to pick another team in case the cards should fall that way and we had to play them. To our surprise, they picked us to alliance with them and we began the playoffs as the number one seed. I want to say that it was a difficult task, but in the most humble of fashions the victory was somewhat poetic in a way. There was no fuss and no contest. It was as if God said we had endured enough turmoil and that he was going to prepare the road for us. As the students won the High Desert League Championship, and raised the trophy high, I looked over at the parents of the students and became overwhelmed with emotion, but did my best not to show it. I was so happy for them. For our team. For our school and for myself. It was proof that our hard work was recognized and that we had evidence to show how far we had come. The students began to hug their parents and family members as we celebrated the victory. Little did I know that it was only the beginning.

I had made an agreement with my wife that I was going to be more present at our son's weekend functions due to missing plenty of soccer games and weekend family events due to Robotics and SkillsUSA competitions. It was creating a very stressful homelife and I wanted desperately to make it right somehow. I spoke to some of the parents who were involved in our program to help me with this and they agreed that they could take on some of the responsibility that I had in making sure the proper arrangements were made for each competition. After winning the High Desert League, there was another competition at the Google Headquarters in Mountain View, California that the students felt they could win. I told them that if they wanted to attend, they would have to work it out with their parents and that I would not be able to attend. The competition was on New Year's Eve weekend. The amount of stress upon my life at the time was somewhat overwhelming because I felt that I wasn't being a good father to my sons by not being there for them and I was not being a good teacher because I wasn't with my students during one of the most important tournaments of their lives. I prayed a lot trying to find peace about these decisions, and anxiety began to creep in. I was not getting sleep and found myself dwelling too much on things that really did not affect me. Aside from all of this, the time came and the students left to Google while I stayed with my family and enjoyed our winter break. I hadn't heard from any of the parents in a couple of days and wondered what had happened over the weekend. I knew they were traveling back home and was sure someone would call me. As I started to enjoy the time with my family, on New Year's Eve, my phone began to ring. It was Jennifer, Adam's mom, explaining to me that the students and the families wanted to come by and say hello and show me something. I asked my wife if that would be OK and she said it was and so the students and their families traveled to my home instead of theirs for New Year's Eve. Hearing the cars pull up made me feel emotionally secure because both my robotics family and my own family, and extended family, were all in one place. As everyone came in, the students said they had a surprise for me. They began presenting me with trophies. Championship trophies. They had won the Google Tournament. Specifically, Xavier and Kyndal who were the first to win for our school. They had done it. In addition, the parents told me that it wasn't just the fact that they had won, but that all three of our teams that had gone to Google to compete had made it to the finals. This meant that regardless of the outcome, we were coming away victorious. We laughed and hugged as I looked at all the hardware they had brought home. I was in shock and in disbelief. They had also brought home the Design and Excellence awards as well, which were given to the team with the best overall design and to the robot which displayed the best overall performance at the competition. It was a beautiful day. As we said our goodbyes, and the families began to leave, I wondered why, for a moment, this was all happening. I couldn't help but think, could he really be showing me how much he loves me? Could God really do these things like rewarding people who do good? My desire was always to make a difference in this world. Even when I was a boy, I wanted to make my mother proud by doing something she could raise her hand in agreement with. Could this be the moment I live that visualization?

Over the course of the season, from middle school and high school, we competed in eight VEX Robotics tournaments. Of those eight, we won seven; and of those tournaments, we had a combined match record of 75 wins and five losses. We advanced to the California State Championship in both middle school and high school and had one of the highest win percentages at the tournaments. In the weeks leading up to the tournament, the students wanted to do try and build a new robot that was an improvement from what we currently had and for whatever reason the design that they were working on wasn't coming together as quickly and as efficiently as they had hoped. There was also another problem that was happening as well. My son, Caleb, had advanced to the Regional Championships for his All Star Soccer team and his games were going to be on the same weekend as the State Championship. Once again, I felt extreme anxiety because I wanted to be a great father and support my son, but felt terrible because I wasn't going to be able to attend one of the biggest days of my students' lives.

The day before the competition, the students and I were in the classroom and they were discussing with themselves that the new robot did not function correctly and that they were not going to do well at the competition. I felt God telling me that Iris was going to be perfectly fine for the competition and that he was going to prepare the way for them. I told the students that I was extremely proud of how far they had come and asked them if they'd be willing to pray with me. They all agreed to and I led our team in prayer. I asked God to bless them not for me but for their sake. That they would see his hand on their lives and that they would know he gave them this victory to show them that he is with them. We packed up our stuff for the competition and I left to Bakersfield and they traveled to Pomona for the State Championship. I had peace that day that whatever happened, I did the right thing, but I had no idea how things were going to turn out.

Saturday came and while in Bakersfield I wondered if their decision making was going well. We had two teams, Kyndal and Xavier's team as well as Cody and Bryce's team. Both were exceptional. I watched my son's soccer teams lose to more advanced soccer teams and I couldn't help, but visualize the parallel between the two and if my students were outmatched. I gave up on the stress of both of the events and just decided I was going to be happy with what transpired. Regardless of the outcome. At about 4 o'clock in the afternoon, my phone rang and it was Jennifer, Adam's mother. The noise on the phone was so loud I could barely hear what was happening. Her voice sounded like a mix of tears and laughter all in one. I asked her immediately what happened. She simply said, "They won!" I was in shock, so I asked her, "What do you mean they won?" She said, "Denny they won the State Championship!" The smile on my face was uncontrollably big. I couldn't believe it. Tears began to roll down my face as I covered my eyes in astonishment while at the same time hearing the students call my name on the other end. They were all gathered on speaker phone letting me know they had accomplished something we had never done. "We did it," they kept saying. "Mr. V. we just won the whole dang thing," they said. I imagined their faces holding up the trophy and raising the banners like we had seen the year before. But as I started listening to their story of how it all came to be, it was clear that God had prepared the way in spite of the obstacles that were presented. The students account of the events began with them getting lucky through the qualifying matches. They said that they were winning matches by a margin of one to five points. Some of the matches they should have lost they said. One match, in particular, the opponents had a full stack and placed it in the 10-point zone which would have given the other team the win had the stack not fallen after the buzzer had sounded. In addition to all of this, during alliance selection they were the third ranked alliance. They chose not to pick our own school because they felt that they had a high chance of winning the tournament with another team. Xavier, Kyndal and Shamir were heartbroken over this as well as the parents. I wished that there were an easier way, but I had explained to the students all year that alliance picking should never be based on friendship. Regardless, they should pick the team that gives them the best chance to win. Cody, Bryce and Fernando chose to follow this and were denied by the top 10 teams because the teams said that Iris was not good enough. They chose a team in 13th place and another in 33rd. It turned out that their decision was correct in the end because the top two alliances in the tournament were disqualified due to an infraction of the rules involving modifications to their robots. Our school advanced to the semifinals when all of this took place and, as a result of the other teams' disqualifications, the semifinals for our team became the finals of the entire tournament. God had made a way where there wasn't one. After hearing the story, I chuckled to myself because to anyone else it would have looked weird to see all of it happen. The students and I knew what we prayed for and it was given in the most dramatic fashion.

My son's soccer team had lost their final matches on Saturday and, as a result, we were able to come home early. Middle School's State Championship was Sunday so I decided not to tell the kids I was coming, but would attend the event and surprise them. I arrived just in time to see what God was doing. Upon arriving to the event, I witnessed our middle school team win the California State Championship. It was one of the most vindicating times for our school because the year before they had been robbed of the opportunity. Colin was able to get back what was taken from him. The feeling it gave me was unreal. I felt like I was dreaming and that things couldn't possibly get any better than this. The tears of joy and smiles of happiness on the kids' faces were so priceless. I felt so amazing to see all of this not only unfold but to see the emotion that followed after all that we had been through. But we weren't done yet.

California State Educator of the Year

During the following week, I received an email from the California League of High Schools that I had been nominated out of thousands of teachers to be the region 10 educator of the year for San Bernardino and Riverside Counties. The information provided said that the nomination had to be given by a district official, principal or county official. I did not know who gave the recommendation but my wife, father, sister, step mother and principal attended the dinner. I was asked to write a speech about my journey and what it meant. I was extremely nervous about speaking. I knew that I wasn't going to feel good about it unless I spoke directly from the heart. So, naturally, I started from the beginning. Much like how I've done here in this book. It was extremely difficult to get through the speech because of the realization of how far I have come as a human being, a father and an educator. After a few hours of amazing speeches from other educators, a winner was chosen. As the speaker said my name, I couldn't believe what was happening. I was being blessed among men and the joy in my heart was overwhelming. After the event concluded, I was told that I was going to be invited to Sacramento to have an opportunity to speak one more time in hopes of becoming the California State Educator of the Year. A few weeks later, my family and I traveled to Sacramento where an even larger committee of Education officials and teachers would listen to my story and decide if I was worthy. As I gave the speech, I couldn't believe the magnitude and size of the conference. My wife looked on as I obsessed about what I was going to say and how I was going to say it. She kept reminding me that I need to stick to the topic, but also say everything from my heart because that's what got me here. After listening to others give their speeches and delivered my own speech, I felt as though, regardless of what the outcome was, my father was extremely proud of who I was and what I had become. The fact that we were there and that his son was being recognized was a giant victory for him because of all the struggle we had gone through when I was a little boy. I could see in his face that his joy and pride in who I was to him was everything. He was beyond proud.

Walking into the auditorium the following day was a nervous experience. There were so many good educators who gave such eloquent speeches and impacted their students so much that I doubted I would be considered. When the announcer began to introduce the California State Educator of the Year, and my name was announced,

I could hear my father's roar of joy, my sisters yell in triumph, my kids cheers of joy my stepmom and my wife's screams. For a moment, time seemed to literally stand still as I could feel the crowd of a couple thousand people stand to their feet in applause and admiration. I had won a great victory, but it wasn't the California State Educator of the Year. It was victory of statistics and probability. The idea and facts that showed that a kid with my background and heartbreak could not grow up to be a successful man who impacts the world in some way. My story was mine alone and its triumph was a symbol of victory for those like me. It was a victory for my students who believed that their teacher was not just a man who taught them educational concepts. It proved to everyone that I was not forgotten and the only person that knew I needed that was HIM. He's known me and I know Him. And to feel that victory around me as I walked toward the stage to accept my award meant a great deal to everyone around me. My hope is that the story I've told inspires everyone who reads it to work beyond their limits. To understand that dreams and aspirations are not only attainable, but they can be real. "Hard work beats talent, when talent doesn't work hard."